D1622621

III. *Sequestered Light*

The Autumn House Poetry Series
Michael Simms, editor

The
Divine
Salt

To Laura
Best wishes !

The Divine Salt

poems by
Peter Blair

Autumn House
Press

© 2003 Peter Blair

All rights reserved. No part of this book can be reproduced in any form whatsoever without written permission from the publisher, except in the case of brief quotations embodied in critical essays or reviews. For information contact Autumn House Press, 87-1/2 Westwood Street, Pittsburgh PA, 15211.

"The Mental Hospital Garden" (17-line excerpt) by William Carlos Williams, from *Collected Poems 1939-1962*, Volume II, © 1948, 1962 by William Carlos Williams. Reprinted by permission of New Directions Publishing Corp.

The cover portrait of St. Francis with stigmata is by Cimabue, late 13th century.

"Autumn House" and "Autumn House Press" are registered trademarks owned by Autumn House Press, a non-profit corporation whose mission is the publication and promotion of poetry.

Text and cover design: Kathy Boykowycz
Editorial Consultant: Eva Maria Simms
Marketing Consultant: Michael Wurster

Printed in the USA
ISBN: 0966941977
Library of Congress Control Number: 2003110472

This book is dedicated to all the patients and staff of St. Francis Hospital's psychiatric ward.

Contents

Acknowledgments

Grateful acknowledgment is made to the following magazines for publishing these poems, some with different titles and in slightly different form:

The And Review: "Driving Home"
The Bassettown Review: "Skeleton Key"
The Birmingham Review: "St. Michael's Cemetery"
5AM: "Freight Train"
The Pittsburgh *Post-Gazette*: "Full House"
poetrymagazine.com: "Love at Mach One"

"Friday for the River" won the 1992 Laurel Arts Poetry Contest sponsored by Laurel Arts Poetry Center, Somerset, Pa.

Stories about St. Francis and the language of some of the poems drawn from *The Little Flowers of Saint Francis*, translated from the original Latin and Italian by Raphael Brown, New York: Doubleday, 1958.

I am grateful to the Pennsylvania Council on the Arts for poetry fellowships which aided in the completion of some of these poems.

I'd like to thank the following people and organizations for their assistance and careful reading of many of these poems: Jack Myers, George O'Brien, Sandee Umbach, the Charlotte Writer's Club, and especially, Elizabeth Gargano. I'd like to thank Michael Simms for his belief in this project and his insightful editorial suggestions.

They are careless
        under the license of the disease
                which has restricted them
to these grounds.
        St. Francis forgive them

        ....

        The light
                is sequestered there
by these enclosing walls.
        They are divided
                from their fellows.
It is a bounty
        from a last year's bird's nest.
                St. Francis,
who befriended the wild birds,
        be their aid,
                those who
have nothing.

                    William Carlos Williams,
                    "The Mental Hospital Garden"

THESE
ENCLOSING
WALLS

Driving to Work

Across the river, St. Francis Hospital
looms above Bloomfield,
two wings of burnt brick, its medieval
spire a dark candle flame.
I've seared my mind in its heat:
belted men to a steel bed
in the seclusion room, walked them
out of electroshock, clinging
to my arm. I've listened to their stories
in narrow confessional rooms.

I park on Penn Avenue
under the hospital's brown shadow.
Above me, pigeons veer
in a wide circle, their angled wings
appear, then disappear.
They nest under these slate eaves
of sorrow, touched by clouds.
The patients have their own names for it:
Saint Frig-it-all, Hell on Pills,
Crazy Eight, Edge City, The Tomb.

Donna Lee Polito

Burt Reynolds wheels over dirt roads
on the movie screen. He escapes the sheriff
who murdered his brother in a Louisiana bayou.
Donna Lee walks slow, head down, willing herself
shadow-like along the opposite wall.
I catch her by the door: *Ready to go?*

She flashes me her full-lipped smile framed
by dark cropped hair, takes my arm, nudges me
with her shoulder: *Burt's not my type.*
When she walks down the first floor hall,
I follow her footsteps as if I were.

This is her first time off the locked floor
in months. Two weeks ago the doctor canceled
her constant watch freeing her
from white dorm walls and cigarette-burned carpet.
She's tried suicide five times in three years:
sleeping pills, tranquilizers, a bathroom razor.
Perhaps she's not thinking of it. She's been fine
for weeks: *helpful, bright,* written on her chart.

I don't see her watching *Exit* signs,
and bright sun-slashes of escape
through window blinds. Lulled, I don't remember
her chilled empty eyes the first day: *I'm going
to do it.* People bunch around the elevator
grumbling in the art deco lobby.
I press the button, turn. Her foot disappears
from the closing light of the front door.

Halfway across the lot at full speed,
she races. I close the gap to ten yards
before she makes the heavy traffic on Penn.
Even then I have no idea. I call the nurse's desk,
thinking she's headed for a bar
like John last week, who ducked out
of X-ray to get drunk at Del's.

Now I know the Angel of Death
is all duty and little risk, all excuse
and little action. My shift stretches out
like a green corridor of rooms, full
of in-patients, urine reductions, blood
pressures, and what a doctor once called,
the grindstone of human suffering—-
until Denny Harper taps my shoulder:
They want you on eight, now.

He nods, as if ducking a punch, avoids
my eyes like bad luck. Behind me, aides whisper.
Sully gives me a wide berth in the elevator.
The doors open on a circle of faces:
the head nurse, a social worker from nine,
a burly detective in a rain coat.
I shake my head. The supervisor nods.

From the eighth floor windows, nurses watched
her run, a tiny wavering figure, escaping
all of us as police cars converged.
She jumped this time, vaulting
over the red railing from the high cement
of the Bloomfield Bridge down
to railroad tracks and scrubby trees.

Skeleton Key

Ben walks the hall, allowed
one cigarette. I'm about to ask him
to try sleep again, when a call
for an admission comes. All five men
from the wing go for a patient—full
restraints. In the tunnel under the street,
going to the ER, we push a carriage loaded
with sheets and belts. The guard rails
clang over our forced wisecracks.

The police found him wandering the streets,
pissing on the federal building.
I fill in his chart: *37 year-old, male Caucasian,*
married, a history of schizophrenia, acts out.
His vacant, belligerent eyes are casualties
not listed on the work-up sheet. *Mr. Heally?*
When we lay hands on his hands, he doesn't resist.
He sees the odds, knows the ritual
of indignities he's about to suffer.

On eight, we wheel him into the quiet room—
blank walls, a bed bolted to the floor:
one belt around his waist, fastened
to each side rail, an anklet belted
to the foot rest, wristlets on each hand, buckled
to the waist belt—injection. The day shift
will get him up. *Watch this,* he leers, spits
straight up. A hocker splats on the caged
light bulb. I turn it off. *Try to sleep.*
Go fuck yourself from the dark room.

Lunch at 4 a.m., I welcome the bland
sobriety of a cafeteria, two elbows
on a white table, coffee. We talk of raises,
a day nurse someone says is *just as crazy
as the patients*, how many shock treatments
Ben's had, no one very interested. Later,
on each patient's chart I write nurse's notes,
the medical catch-words as apt for me
as the patients: *manipulative, preoccupied,
tense, testing limits*. Doleful as brakes
of a slowing truck, Mr. Heally groans,
awake behind double doors.

Through mesh I tell him where he is.
He's groggy, asks to piss. I get a urinal,
guide him, empty it, then light a cigarette,
hold the filter tip to his lips like a war movie.
Just a man, without a name-tag,
or the three keys: the short one for the elevator,
the big one for the stairwells, the long one
for the belt locks, and no access
to the skeleton key in a safe behind the desk,
for the steel window screens, eight flights.

My Job

His slippers flop, clop, the shiny linoleum,
white and streaked with smears of light.

Go right, Mr. Heally. The X-ray room's
lined by steel chairs gleaming along the wall.

He keeps walking straight. I call his name, lightly
touch his elbow. He jerks it away, paces fast:

I'm out of here. The street door opens around him,
then shuts, snuffing the sunshine along its edges.

When he vanishes, it's Donna Lee
running out into the light again. I sprint

down the hall, bang open the door: *Mr. Heally,
I'll lose my job.* I feel the freedom, the open

air in mid-shift, the raw permission
of the street. He stops, shoulders slumping,

Really? For an instant, caught in sunlight,
we hesitate. His shirt's untucked. The hot sidewalk

burns through his slippers. Hands in my pockets,
sheepish, I finger my keys, nod, shrug.

A truck grinds by us. He slowly shuffles back,
eyes on the squared-off sky above walls of brick.

Lunch Break Between Wings

I kick through decayed leaves
on the sidewalk, scudding,
crackling.

A breeze tumbles them
into the street. Tires
crush them.

I smell their tannic acid, the musty,
pungent scent
of autumn.

In the cold wind, slanted
sunlight knifes over
the low rooftops.

A cyclone of leaves and dust whirls,
dances near me, like the blinding
restless grief

she must have felt on the bridge, high
above ragged treetops. Donna Lee,
lost in the air

above the tracks. The rustling wind
dusts my eyes. *Donna Lee,*
don't leave.

The leaves hush their whispers.
A palm-shaped maple
wings across

my hair. I pull it free, drop it
fluttering softly
to the ground.

Instructions for Opening a Window

Open the safe and palm the dumbbell weight
of the steel skeleton key. Hide it walking the hall.
Ask the patient to step out of the room. Scan
for sharp objects. Close the door while your backup
guards the entrance. Insert the key in the box
on the window pane, its hole like a misshapen bell.
Swing open the steel screen, the sash creaking
on its heavy hinges. Close your mind to images
of bodies falling, yourself falling eight floors down
to the stone-studded grass of Allegheny Cemetery.
Breathe in the air high above trees and the mosaic
of square roof tops, gridded by streets. Listen
to Mr. Heally in the next room keening a sweet song
of escape. Close the screen. Hear it clang. Test it.
Gaze at the Allegheny's north shore, an open green hill
in dust and sunlight haze. Realize that you are dust.
Watch the river under clouds move sluggishly
through the gray, crisscrossed, wire mesh.
Hold the key in your closed fist. Open your eyes.

Litany for Edwin

Eyes open, the 18-year-old boy lies stiff
and still on the bed. I whisper, *Edwin,*
it's not so bad. He stares at the ceiling,
as if into a deep sky looking for lost stars
among paint cracks and a beige void.
The world, I mean. I touch a wet cloth
to his sad, pimply face. *Consciousness*
is pleasing, Edwin. Adam says that
in Paradise. He's in the last room at the end
of the unit. If he doesn't wake up soon
they'll ship him to the chronic ward. *Edwin, most*
madness is divinest sense. Like the grief-stricken
friend of a coma patient in a soap opera,
I keep talking: *the best wisdom is only a sublime*
misery. But his sleep is conscious, open-eyed.
The words I throw against a dark window
on lonely nights mean nothing here.
His parents arrive with their own words.
My, my, Edwin dear, my, my, his mother
murmurs. Thin, shrugging, apologetic,
she tucks and smoothes the sheet. I leave him
to his wide-eyed sleep, wondering where he goes
in dreams: to the elf forest of Rivendell,
or to the moon where Jung's patient fled
for years to escape her incestuous brother,
or any world, free of bare walls and the pure
white sheet stretched over his motionless body.

Angel Dust Devil

Inside the quiet room, Clifford broods
on the bed. His dinner tray's heavy in my hands,
compartments neatly filled: meat loaf,
Jello, mashed potatoes. I knock lightly.
Dinner time, I say softly. From everywhere
Clifford's yell echoes in the enclosed space
booming, voluminous, sustained
for three seconds: *Get ooouutt!*
I drop and catch the tray, surprised,
at my trembling hands, the shock slammed
into my central nervous system.
Aides don't get angry, don't want the hard chunk
of their knuckles on Clifford's mouth.
In my mind I see the flat bottom of the heavy tray
smashing down on his back. Only the teary pain
in his face stops me. It's his third admission
in six months since taking tainted angel dust.
I walk out slowly, lock the door.
No dinner for Clifford, from me, tonight.

Saint Francis Night Shift

I'm not an M.D., thumbing through
his charts of "fruits and nuts,"
his diagnoses, a mishmash of gut feelings
and "classic cases": neuroses,
psychoses, and whatever he chooses to see.
I'm not a nurse, caretaker goddess,
her uniform pure white as the pills
rattling in the Dixie cups at meds time;
not a saint like Francis,
putting it all on the line for God;
or Charles who was admitted
for walking the Fort Pitt Tunnel's
yellow line at rush hour
so he could see Pittsburgh
emerge from smog and darkness.

I'm an aide, but who do I aid,
holding a patient down,
as the nurse peels jeans and underwear
to expose the white flank of buttock
to the needle? How do I aid?
I sit on the quiet room floor
as Mr. Heally lies strapped to the bed.
Don't worry, I tell him, *I'm the only thing*
on the walls besides the paint.

Head down, muttering, John paces
in his "powder keg" walk.
Give St. Francis a chance, I say,
knowing I've revealed to the staff
his dark thoughts, his hands around
his mother's throat. *It's out of our hands.*
It's our job. It's not for us to say,
we aides mumble at the bar after the shift.

Who do I aid but myself,
a go-between, a mere assistant
in this emergency room of the mind,
this eighth floor world, suspended
between the streets and the state
mental institution? If John told me
he talked to birds, like St. Francis,
would I report that to the doctors?

Doctor Strong

Everyday the psych aides page Dr. Strong
though he doesn't exist. He appears in minutes
on any of twelve floors: five to ten of us
circle the patient and close in. Sometimes
he wears a badge, carries a nightstick, a gun.
One Sunday when Tally threatens
to beat my head against the wall by the elevator,
Dr. Strong is a weary sergeant
with red-rimmed eyes. *The psychological
approach not working for you?* he says
after he's escorted Tally to the quiet room.
I pour Dr. Strong a cup of coffee, thank him
for coming, though I'm glad to see his back.

Another time Ben pushes an aide into a wall.
He staggers, arms out, comes at me
his face contorted by puffed cheeks
and bulging eyes. I call *Dr. Strong,*
but the aide grabs Ben from behind,
drags him to his restraint chair:
Just a bad reaction to his meds.
Men arrive from seven, nine. *These people
call Dr. Strong when a patient sneezes.*

Sometimes I am Dr. Strong: my hands pin
elbows and forearms, or pry a patient's hand
from an aide's neck. I grab his pinky and peel
firmly back as I learned from nurse Dougherty,
who tells us, *If someone messes with you
they're messing with Dr. Strong.*
At Western Psych, they call him Dr. Force,
but patients recognize him all the same.

Psychiatric Chess

*It is a matter of discovering how to pass between the rages which
displace each other in tender parallels, or how to pass under the
shaggy undulations through which terrors are well retained.
We yearn for the obscure thrusts of our beginning which enclosed us
in humid walls. —Matta*

Back from weekend break, I see Ray on Eight East
on crutches, depressed. His pantleg cut away,
a thick white bandage winds around his thigh.
Hey *Pezz,* he calls, slouching onto the bed.
Long ago he nicknamed me *Peasant* because
You work too much and play too little.
He tells me the story, a Thorazine glaze in his eyes.

Out of work for five months, he tried one last time.
The Pizza World clerk eyed his torn t-shirt,
shook his head with a sneer. Ray lunged
across the counter: *Kiss my ass,* he growled,
as the guy reached under the counter,
lifted a gun. *Come on, asshole, shoot.*
The barrel lit up. The gun spit fire. The bullet
ripped his thigh inches from his groin. Ray smiled,
limped away into the Bloomfield darkness.

He challenges me to chess as usual. The pieces
of the unit's board depleted, we use spare change
for pawns. His queen's an overturned
medication cup. I drop in between duties,
make my moves. As usual, I lose.
He shrugs: *Chess is simple. Life's what's hard.*
Control, he adds, *control each square, two, three
ways: rook, bishop, queen in the background.*

As a boy I ran through the streets of Point Breeze
knocking over garbage cans with Ray and George,
the Blossick boys. I take up a collection
among friends, buy him an electronic chess set.
A crenellated wall of knights and pawns
surrounds the board. He plays all day,
beats the computer's master level.
Someone steals it after a week.

In the next three years, he'll jump off
the Sixth Street Bridge into the river
and live, join and leave the seminary,
marry and divorce, take 28 sleeping pills.
In his father's house, he'll sleep
like a child on the bed in his small square,
third-floor room, a Roberto Clemente poster
on the wall, old board games on a shelf.

Walter

Warts cover his face, disappear
into his shirt, his cheeks and neck
bubbled like bread dough.
But he's good with the patients.
Perhaps they trust him
because his skin's gone mad. Married
22 years, he sends his son to college
on a St. Francis paycheck. Tonight
he teaches me the logic of restraint belts:
the flat little dagger of steel
slips into the belt lock.
A click of his key loosens the strap,
pinched tight by the metal hammerhead.
His gentle hands close over mine,
show my fingers how.

In the quiet room, a new admission
loses his bowels in the bed.
*I'm glad you're not afraid
to get shit on your hands,*
Walter tells me. *Not like most
of these aides.* We lift sheets
in our palms, cup them carefully
around the warm turds,
tilt them over the bedpan.
We clean the patient with wet
wash cloths. *What would my dad
think of me now?* I joke. *He'd be glad
he didn't have to do it,* Walter says.

Without Walter, I wouldn't know
the mysterious warmth
and weight of a turd
through a pillow case, the assurance
of gentle hands on a patient's body,
or the quiet click
that unlocks restraints.

Courtyard

Roses, fire-truck red
and studded with thorns,
reach fluted petals around my bench.
The high stone wall behind me
topped with barbed wire
encloses the yard. I lay out
fluted petals of ham
beside the white bread.
The shiny apple's round
red eye sees all: the patients
at their games, the bricks,
the cyclone fencing
wrapped around its curved
glowing world.

Two men play basketball.
Others wander in the sunlight,
dispassionate on lunch hour.
A boy enters the cafeteria door,
disappears up to his room.
In this garden, nuns
walk in the evening. Aides smoke
on break. The pathways glisten
with pebbles, inviting a stroll
under the twin stone smiles
of St. Francis and the Virgin Mary.

John leaps, takes a shot.
His forearm catapults the ball,
and it arcs, descends
splashes into the cords.
He's in for depression,
a two-week admission.
For only an instant, the net
grips the ball's curved temples,
then lets it fall to the asphalt.

THE LICENSE
OF THE
DISEASE

Golden Clay

By the elevator door, Vicki Di Salvo,
leans against the Formica counter
of the nurse's station: *How about a light, darling?*
A new patient, sexy in tight sweats,
blond, a Lauren Bacall look-alike, she wiggles
her cigarette between fingers, her elbow
propped on the counter. I hesitate.
She sashays towards me. *Well, honey?*

I'm hypnotized by her hips, her fantasy,
her presence, some casino bar,
high above Pittsburgh's Golden Triangle.
She's enjoying it, and I'm trapped
in her game. Chuck at the desk,
sees my mystified eyes: *Vicki, you've had
your one cigarette for the morning.* Her face clouds
into a sneer: *One, two, three . . .*

What is real but her need
to pretend the fantasy, and tender it
to me? My mother danced
in her bedroom, cupping a wine glass.
She swayed to the radio
before descending to make hot chocolate
for six kids in the kitchen,
living the fantasy she gave up for us.
Vicki's always going to be a woman
to someone, but this is the unit
where the bar dispenses pills, prescriptions
for disaster: no footrail, gleaming
counter, or glittering mirrors
to reflect her golden hair.

Once, St. Francis saw a lady statue
in a vision: a golden head, silver torso,
iron thighs and clay feet. His holy order,
she told him, would begin in gold
and turn into clay. That day, I slink off
to the coatroom on feet of clay,
too flustered to hear what my vision
will say, when she gets to *ten*.

Ed's New Place

Loud disco vibrates loose window panes
and a drunken conga line thuds
floorboards. We grab each others' hips
a little too hard. A few light up reefers
in corners. Couples disappear
as the late hours fade into a drowsy fog.
I'm with Diane, a psych nurse.
She recites Zooey's last speech to Franny:
Everyone is Jesus, every patient.
Give me a break, Ed mutters,
and hands me another beer.

I promise Diane a ride home, open
the bedroom door for our coats.
It's Hieronymous Bosch's vision,
the bedroom of earthly delights:
curled naked bodies paired, sprawled,
on the crowded bed, the blanketed floor.
Limbs intertwined, soft skin undulates,
flickers in the dim doorway light.
Their moans, giggles, breathe
ecstasy, muffled in smoky air.

I click the door shut on the quiet ceremony,
the innocent skin. *What's wrong?*
Diane asks, her perfume close
around my shoulders. *Nothing,* I say.
Let's have another beer.

Love in the Closet

I hear his soft singing, an Eagles' tune,
Looking for a lover who won't
blow my cover, inside his room.
I stop at female giggles, whispers,
his door suspiciously cracked. Inside,
they're kissing in the closet nook.
He has her up against shelves,
his hand inside her shirt. He smiles,
slowly backs away as Vicki slips by me
into the hall. *15-minute penalty*, he says.
Illegal use of hands. I'd seen him
in the lounge lean over the chair arm
next to him. Vicki sat straight up,
head back, avoiding his eyes
but listening. He says he can't help it:
Under those tight jeans, I know
there's a sweet pussy. We have him
for a few days of psychiatric evaluation,
a stalking case. Closing his eyes, long hair
hanging back, he sees something steamy
and dark beyond his eyelids, smells
more than Spic and Span. He breathes
deep: *Yielding thighs, man.*
The nurse transfers him to 801,
nearest the front desk, forbids him
the female side, and ties
his door open with a restraint belt.

Numbers

Mr. Steele flicks the cards down on the desk,
clicks them off his fingertips. The cards line up
in columns, random kings waiting to rule
their lower numbers in perfect solitaire.
He scans his fingers: *My digits.* He's dealt poker
for 20 years. *Where would I be*
without my precious 10. He loves Vegas casinos,
especially craps. He bets "no pass" every 7
7's. I ask him to make his bed. He calculates
odds: *Cut you for it, low number slaves.*

He started pushing football pools in high school,
the cafeteria at lunch, made 5 thousand dollars
in 1 year, almost as much as his father.
With a sheepish grin he asks me to smuggle
a bottle of Johnny Walker. He takes red label
when he wins, black on a losing streak.
Tell Dr. Twerski I'll beat that casino, come back,
and buy this hospital. He's got a formula
to beat the booze: 7 drinks every 3 hours.

10 minutes later his bed's not made.
We face off over the rumpled sheets dragging
on the floor, the mattress half visible.
He cocks his head, still as a bird. But his eyes shift,
flicking to his bed, to me at the door,
to the red and black numbers on the cards.

The Party

I've held brains in my hands,
Jim Staub tells me over shouts, laughter,
and a stereo banging guitar chords. He sits
cross-legged on the lowest step, bearded,
scraggly-haired, a young face, old eyes.
The stairway's strewn with the bodies
of overcoats, down jackets.

No one knows what I've seen.
His friends' guts splattered on jungle leaves
at the LZ ambush. He played dead
in a pool of blood gathering in the long grass.
SHE doesn't know. It's her party,
Jeanie, the sandy-haired psych nurse, his ex-wife.
A crazed smile spreads across his face,
his teeth like bullets lined up in a clip.

Make me a sandwich! He stomps
to the kitchen, opens the fridge.
Their divorce is almost final,
his kids tucked away at Jeanie's mom's.
His night-mopper, janitor job at the City-
County Building looms in a few hours.
Explosions and machine-gun fire
will echo in his mind, down the empty
hallways past the locked, name-plated doors
to the marble vestibule of the mayor's office.

Fuck all of you, he yells. The party stops.
Sue, the nurse who got the lawyer,
stands between them. Jimi Hendrix blares
in the utter silence, *If six turned out to be nine.*
Please go, Jeanie says. *The war's over.*
He's blackened her eye once before,
and the light goes out in front of him
as he slams the fridge, and smashes his glass
onto the tile floor. *Yes, go,* Sue holds
his army jacket out by the arms.
If this were the unit, they'd have him
in the quiet room. But there's only outside:
the porch, the street, his empty apartment.

No one, no one, no one. His words boom
like shots. We're ready to grab him,
afraid of his trembling, and the slow
deliberate shaking of his down-turned head.
He wheels around and snatches his coat.
The front door slams behind him.
On the porch, he crashes into a lawn chair,
swivels, hurls a potted plant at the door,
then staggers, hands out, down the steps,
his footfalls growing fainter.

Midnight

Strapped down in the seclusion room,
he needs a bed pan. When he arches his body,
the gown falls away: A scar above his hip,
a jagged welt, ripples as he breathes.
He angles his head into the pillow, stares,
not sure I'm there. His bowels bring him back
to St. Francis Hospital from Viet Nam,
a reassuring smell, our common connection.

A series of "red" episodes, flashbacks,
reassigned him here from the VA hospital.
The lithium shot minutes ago keeps him distant,
like his name, Angel, above the world
of his past. I clean him with warm washcloths,
towels spread under him to save the sheet.

Who are you? His sidelong eyes peek at me
from around a corner of air.
You think I can't break these belts?
I hope you don't try, I answer,
carry the bedpan toward the door. *Don't go,*
he commands, a desperate sergeant.
The mayhem if he loses it will be worse
than the tension or fecal smell. So I slide
my back down against the wall, sit on the floor.

Everyone hates midnight, seven more hours
of darkness to go. They made him point man
on patrols. *Six shades of green and ten paces*
into infinity. A sniper got him in the side
on his thirtieth mission. The injection
steadily lulls him from talk to sleep.
For twenty minutes, I crouch in the jungle,
and I don't move a muscle.

Full House

John's pacing again. In a cloud of smoke,
he grabs the lit cigarette hanging
from Rock's chapped lips, stubs it out
on a chair arm. *Send me to another floor,*
Rock says, *or I'll kill that SOB.*
Two new admissions slouch off
the elevator. One's sallow-faced, quiet,
probably an alcoholic. The other, a psychotic,
darts angry glances at Rock who grouses:
I wish they'd hang "No Vacancy"
in the emergency room. We have a full house,
on a gray Sunday in December.
Rock, I say, *we wouldn't trade you,*
for two receivers and a quarterback.
I heard that once in a play, and Rock's chart
said he played semi-pro football
in his youth. *Come on, the game's on.*
In the lounge, the Steelers play
the hated Raiders: *the Snake, the Assassin.*
We cheer as the announcer crows: *Jack Splat*
with a sweet hit, and groan at a blown
interference call against us. More patients
gather, women from the other end of the unit,
until we're twenty strong. *That's a penalty,*
or my name ain't Joe! the alcoholic yells,
standing, pointing at the black and white
fuzzy picture. *Yeah,* we thunder,
and Rock nicknames him, *Ref.*
In the back by the window, John smiles.

Franco breaks one for the final score,
ices it, and we all go crazy. Cheering
in a madhouse, Rock leads a victory dance
around the pool table. I join in,
gyrating, high-fiving as we pass
the steel window latches, the restraint locker,
and the TV chained to the pillar.

Moving Day

At the bar George and I list
the old litany, his mom's paranoia,
two brothers' depression,
Ray's suicide. *When's my turn?* he asks,
then stares into his beer, as if seeing
the doom that's visited his family:
the Blossicks, like the old
Greek House of Atreus.

All day George and I moved our youth
out of the old brick house,
the lacquered table where we played
Fish, Stud-poker, and Risk
at war on a map of the world.
Wrestling an overstuffed chair
through the narrow porch door,
we sidestepped, turned, and
shifted as its padded arms
prodded our sides. Hardy weeds
sprouted like madness
through cracks in the cement steps.

George's father rubbed a dresser-top,
finding invisible scratches
as he superintended his own exit.
By the truck, he grabbed my hand. Tears
welled in his eyes, his lips quavered:
You can only do so much.
Together we watched Ray's furniture
lying scattered in the tall grass
in the sunlight. We left the table
overturned by the curb, its back cracked,
bearing forgotten initials.

Banging the Dog

Rain raps on the tar paper roof of the hunting camp.
George Blossick's in the dog, his used Corolla,
Beckle in his pick-up behind him,
250-pound stomach pressed against the wheel.
We're bleary-eyed from beer and boredom,
the woods around the cabin curtained off
by rain: no shots, no deer. All weekend
we've jagged Blossick about the dog.
With each case of Iron, we christened it again:
She's a junker. A rust-bucket on wheels.
A used up piece of petrified dinosaur shit.

Now Beckle gurgles a deep laugh,
revving the pick-up. He shoves it into drive
and bangs the dog from behind.
Blossick's head snaps back on impact, waving
frantically to stop him, but Beckle has an audience.
Bang her again, boy, we egg him on.
He knocks into the dog, grinning
a toothy leer, mad for distraction and sleep
like his truck's grill and fogged headlights.

The helpless white hatchback jerks forward,
squealing through its brakes each time.
Beckle howls in the cab. Blossick swings
his legs out of the car door, stands
among the cheering men. He shakes his head,
still a good sport, his grin slipping. *Bang.*
The bumper hangs down. *Bang.* The back dents.
Bang. The dog's muffler-pipe falls
into grass like a tail between its legs.

That's it. Get the fuck out of that truck!
Blossick rips open the door so fast
it springs back shut. He wrenches the handle,
pulls Beckle out, drags him through wet grass,
raises his fist as the others pull him away.
Beckle lies still, docile, rain pelting his face.
Inspecting the dog's back end,
Blossick yells that *he's* not paying
for a new bumper, and that the dog better start
or some asshole's going to tow it
with his pick-up all the way to Elfinwild.

His hoarse voice rises and falls
like a man giving himself directions
so he won't forget, or a man talking to himself
after an accident he helped cause.
It's a song he wants us to hear,
even the trees and squat, brooding metal trucks
up to their chins in tall grass.
Over the steady drumming of drops
on the hoods, we hear his love
for the beat-up dog, see his rage.
Through our drunk stupor, we feel the rain.

Steel Church

Jack Ramsey punches out an orderly,
hurls a food tray like a discus
at waiting doctors, and breaks for the window.
Jack's lowered shoulder hits Ed
in the chest as he races to leap
to a slate overhang, and shinny down
a drain pipe. *Dr. Strong* crackles
over the loudspeaker, drowned out by Ed's scream.
Jack breaks Ed's finger getting the skeleton key,
but we five aides drag him to the floor.
I'll get every one of you for this!

In the quiet room, Jack strains against belts,
and a sedative, calls for his doctor,
now in the emergency room for a cut
from a flying food tray. A few days before,
Jack's older brother grabbed him
from behind, pinning his arms, whispering,
Stay here, three days, for mom, for the court,
and I'll get you that new GTO.
High on speed, Jack raced his car
off Cherry Hill Road, leaping into woods.
Just like "Rat Patrol," he said
when the police brought him to us.

St. Francis rebuilt a ruined abbey,
gutted by years of neglect. Brick by brick,
he and his friars raised a spire high
over the Italian hills. Now in a haze of Darvon,
Jack claims he'll make his crashed car,
Just like new, part by part by part.

I leave him in the white room
where his church speeds and roars
on the highway of his brain, the dash
glowing like an altar: speedometer,
tachometer, tabernacles of rotation,
the curved fenders sleek as the marble
shoulders of angels guarding the horsepower
hoarded in the engine's nave.

Francis was not more careful with his abbey
than Jack would be with his Trans Am,
bathing every engine part in solvent,
rebuilding it with the mortar of gaskets
and grease, filling out the body with gobs
of Bondo. Weeks later I see him
in Bloomfield, his head bent in the darkness
under the high arch of the hood.

Riding in the Dog with George Blossick

Don't mind that blue smoke under the hood.
Just oil shooting up through worn valves.
Burns with the gas. Engine's old.
Do you like my radio? Of course, it works.
Turn the bobby pin. Saturday I rewired it,
but didn't leave enough slack.
The music sounds better upside down.
This could be your car. Even trade.
Yours for the dog. I'll throw in 50 bucks.
Last month it started leaking oil, left a trail.
It took me five quarts to get home.
All day I worked on this sucker,
took the engine apart 3 times, got under there
oil dripping in my eyes, stuck a half-moon gasket
up into its crankcase where I couldn't see,
just feel. See that house? I put the roof on it.
Still looks decent after 10 years. Not like the dog.
Brandy told her class, *My daddy's hobby
is junk cars.* Guess where she heard that?
Oh well, that's wife. Keep moving.
That's the secret. I see my dad every Saturday
since his cancer. He stays home,
gets depressed. That's inviting it back.
We hit a bucket of balls, fix something
around the house, talk. He gets these ideas,
like it's his time to go, or he blew it with my mom.
Piss on that. He's got lots of years left.
So, we're swapping cars, right? I'll throw in
25 bucks. Did I say 50 before? Well, it's getting dark.
You won't see the rust spots on the body.

Love at Mach One

mach one: flying at the speed of sound

I wonder if she's thinking about me,
Tom says, accelerating his '76 Corvette
to a hundred. *She's gotta be.*
She had me arrested, right? White lines
flash by like strobes. Reflectors tick on
far out in the dark. We seem to catch
our own headlights. His pilot hands
steady on the wheel, Tom guns the speed again.
See how the front end torques up? What a rush.

The sentry salutes his name tag at the base.
In the Officers' Club, Tom's a celebrity,
grounded until his hearing.
Pilots ask about his case, and drift away.
He's been through silver searches
high above the continent, combat quests,
but no real enemy yet. Flying goes on
in his eyes, skimming clouds in a jet snake
with wings. The drunker he gets,
the more he's on his own.

Hidden in the late hour's squeeze,
between the need to stay and the need
to go home, he tells me he proposed to her
drunk one night in the green cinderblock
hallway of her apartment house,
Hey, baby, let's get married.
Perhaps she saw him then,
a careless feather weighed down with iron,
herself in the cross hairs of his overconfidence.

Perhaps she saw him in flames,
a streak in the desert sky. *No*, she said,
left him standing by the closed door,
no kiss. *Whore*, he screamed,
You're not good enough.

Next day, drunk, on a hop to Las Vegas,
he wrote letters full of angry sex,
sent boxes of roses, dozens of yellow gardenias
to her office back home. She stalked out
when secretaries came to stare
at the bouquets blooming like fire
from the window sills, radiators,
trash cans. Detectives arrested him
at the airport returning.

All day fighter-jets take off behind his yard.
They clear the trees and swoop
straight up into the endless give
of blue until the tiny darts and smoke-
tails disappear. *We're sky-cowboys, died
and gone to heaven up in that cockpit*,
he once said. But now he tosses his keys
across his kitchen counter. It's 3 AM.
He tells me about the letters: *Something
like "if you're really good, I'll let you
lick my rocket"* . . . *You guess the rest.*

Night isn't reasonable.
Tom flies between the moon
and the precocial, throbbing eroticism
of a jet engine. His pals hang out
at the Wild Blue Yonder Lounge

where a plastic rhino's penis
squirts shots of scotch. With a shrug
he looks around: *I'm living the American
Dream.* He has four cars, a workshop,
and king-sized bed where their bodies crashed
against each other like a dogfight
in the sky. *She gave my letters to the cops
and the brass.* A roar vibrates the windows.
Night shift, he says, *testing out
the after-burners on the F-15's.*

Years ago, entranced, in the station wagon,
we listened to Tom shout our dreams.
Our fathers were still alive
and the only love letters Tom had written
were to his future. The 454 engine roared,
hurtled us close to the night sky
above dark Pennsylvania hills.
Heading to our camp, Tom talked of Einstein,
the prince of atoms and novas.
He knew the circumferences and vast diameters
of galaxies. Sighting along his finger,
he showed me the Orion nebula's
huge explosions. We were speeding
toward their dim, silver light.

God's Staircase

The stars are our stepping stones
to heaven, he shouts. Restraint belts
hold his dancing wrists in tight orbit
around the bed rail. His words streak past
at the speed of light: moon shots,
splash-downs, the glory days
when he worked for NASA. Let go
in the seventies, cut loose from dreams
of space stations and manned missions
to Mars, he lies marooned, raging
on the quiet room's manic planet.

After Apollo 13, a reporter asked him
why God didn't build stairs
if he wanted us to reach the moon.
Fool, he yelled, the ecstatic energy
barely contained, smiling, carrying it off
in good humor, *THESE are the stairs.*
Mission control is God's staircase.
His arm swung out to the steps
of the amphitheater, where monitors
and men ringed the moon map,
cratered, swept by vague shadows,
the Sea of Serenity, the Ocean of Storms.

Freight Train

There's always the freight train,
the black and white steel-tube tank cars
and flat-faced boxcars ramming through it all.
There's always the freight train
along the bank, dividing the mountain
from the waves, while a woman vomits
on the levee and a boater pours a fifth
of whiskey overboard when the police boat
gurgles around the bend. There are always
the snub-nosed diesels, back to back,
pulling straggling empty coal cars
into the vanishing point under the bridge.
Someone always looks up at the freight train,
says, *That's a long one*. The red speed boat
guns its motor, races the train, beats it.
You can always beat it to some arbitrary point,
but it keeps going when you tire
of its loaded, lumbering, daily body of rust
and cracked paint. And there's always
another one, not too soon or too late,
plain as the molecules on your face
and you turn away to the young lovers in jeans
rolling on the lawn. She gets up.
He throws a blanket at her.
She swings her bag at him in a slow, hard arc,
walks away. He catches her. She throws
a half-hearted fist that ends in a kiss
that's always too soon, and long.
And then they're on the grass again.
He's between her legs, dry-humping,
before he lets her throw him off
and the freight train bears down on them
from a distant notch between the hills.

Friday for the River

After work, you bring a yellow envelope
stuffed with tips from The Wheel Café.
My check from St. Francis Hospital
bears the saint's image, arms raised in prayer.
This week we had two on suicide watch,
and a schizophrenic wrote his name in shit
on the quiet room wall. We stroll into the cold,
windless evening. It's Friday, an illusion
of completeness upon us. Walking twilit streets
to the river, we pass people jostling home
or cramming into happy hours. Lights switch on
along the wharf, and the sky's muted blue
corona fades behind Coal Hill.

The river gives back everything
the sky sends down. The bridge arcs
into its reflection, a perfect ellipse of girders.
The hill carries its dark complement,
houses clinging to its underbelly. Along West End,
the lamps set down spikes of light
that shiver in the gloom of the river bend,
the water surface invisible. You lean
against me, your eyes luminous
as the blue water. We look over the levee,
down into a stillness that contains us,
a stillness where a red full moon rises
into the depths of the Allegheny.

SEQUESTERED

LIGHT

St. Michael's Cemetery

I've seen it for years from city streets,
high on a green ridge above Pittsburgh's South Side.
Starting from the huge Stroh's clock,
whose heavy wooden hands count the minutes
against a brick wall by the river,
I hike up cement stairs cleated to shale,
past row houses contoured to slopes,
to iron gates caked with shiny black paint.
I follow asphalt between tool sheds
to a hillside studded with smooth tombstones,
and a Virgin Mary, leaning in blue robes.

I sit on a gravestone for the view:
Margaret Frolich, 1888-1977. Her cross fixes
its flat stare on the ridges, as if her life
had ground its way up the steep hill
from the maze of the city below to gaze
at a blue old age where mist reclaims mountains.
Tiny cars gleam around stone hives.
On a fuzzed hill, a spire marks the neighborhood
I was born in, and from here, St. Francis Hospital
is only a pale bunker bathed in haze.

I've come here to see the distance, the angel
perched on a mausoleum. His hollow eyes
show me the view from death: grass
in the foreground, bluish valleys beyond,
and a city's stone face staring skyward.

Storm

*I believe in the future resolution of these two states, dream and
reality, which are seemingly so contradictory, into a kind of absolute
reality, a surreality.* —Andre Breton

This time, as if a storm wind
blows from Clifford's room,
papers fly through the doorway:
sheafs, yellowed and new,
his novel, *The Loneliness
of the Long Distance Psych Patient.*
Clifford sprints the hall, drop-kicks
the elevator door, pounds it. *Dr. Strong,
Eight East.* We aides ring him
at a distance, a magic circle,
a human wall, an audience. Lightning
flashes in his eyes. *Let me out!*
he thunders. We wait in the charged air.
He carries a shiny tube of toothpaste
unscrews the cap, squeezes.
Toothpaste whirls at us,
from his twirling hand, squirting snakes
of white paste like streamers
all around him. *Angel dust,* he yells,
gropes upward at a ceiling bulb,
caged, dull, yellow. *Light!*
We carry his writhing body to the quiet room.
Scraping toothpaste off the carpet,
I hear Clifford's muffled screams in the hall.
His mind is all around me, smeared
on the walls, stuck to the light.

Mantra

Francis knelt by the bed,
weeping after his host
had fallen asleep,
prayed, *My God and my all,*
his mantra, the whole night.
He threw his spirit into the words
as the ghostly seeds
of a dandelion leap into the wind
that bends its stalk
in hard prayer. His host,
pretending to sleep, listened
in shocked rapture all night.

In Saint Francis psych ward,
Mr. Heally lies half off a bed
bolted to the floor. Tangled
in straps, he moans to curtainless,
screened windows: *My God,
I'm all done.* Yesterday, he searched
the phone book for a new doctor,
muttering, *Fucking shock treatments.*
The pages fluttered, rasped.
Thorazine cures dualism.

Now the drugs, the doctors,
splinter like broken glass.
I gaze at him through wire mesh
at 3 a.m. Walter, the other aide, dozes
in the lounge, but like Francis' host,
I can't sleep. I listen to the voice,
the weeping whisper that echoes
in the darkness, the mind
on the other side of dualism.

Changing the Ground

*Science has almost exactly replaced the role that revelation served
in the Middle Ages.* —Houston Smith

Most close their eyes, wait for the lightning
to streak across their retinas
and jolt their toes apart. Their foreheads clang
against the metal headsets after the quick click
of the black switch. As fast as the doctor says, *On,*
it's off. Then their eyes open, REM-blinking.
Their hands twitch under the straps.
The insides of their eyelids shine lava-red.

It's my job to talk them off the carriage,
walk them to a nearby bed and a felt blanket,
cajole them back from a sky of thunderbolts.
From a jumbled fetal comfort, hugging their knees,
they stare up at fluorescent tubes glowing,
faint essence of brain waves above them.

They remind me of the posture and blank eyes
of Pompeians buried alive in amazement
2000 years ago; their carefully excavated eye-sockets
are cool and empty, like the volcano's crater
after the blast, oval windows to their brains,
confused beyond belief, beyond history.

That morning we ride the elevator from eight,
as if down a lava shaft to the second floor.
The patients, quiet, mostly women,
have been there before. Jane, who joined Hare Krishna,
says her parents are looking out for her.
Sandy says she can't talk to her husband
without crying, that she never loved him.

Mrs. Kurpinsky repeats over and over, *I want
to go to bed. I want to go to bed.*

■

Once in Spokane, Washington, a black cloud
rose slowly in the west all day,
reducing the blue sky to a hellish-red
squall-line in the east: no storm, wind or rain.
Streetlights, headlights came on, a May afternoon.
We wandered in the park darkly amazed
by a sky breathless for thunder
and the shock treatment of lightning.

Soon black ash fell softly, silently.
It chalked our hair, tingled our eyelashes,
gritted between our teeth. We ran to the car
collars pulled up over our faces like bandit masks.
The dash glowed dimly, the windshield opaque.
The news said Mount St. Helens had blown
three hundred miles away. We holed up
under twenty-four hour curfew, sealed
the windows against the silent storm,
the blinded squirrels, the dry black air
that tried to bury us alive
for three days, then passed on.

■

We have to pray for a sign, St. Francis said.
Brother Bernard agreed. Two hours they knelt
by the road above the lush Italian valley
in suffocating heat. When night took the sky
by storm, Francis opened the Gospel,
random words above his finger on a page:
Rebuild my fallen church. Next day he changed
the ground with brick and stone.

Sandy smiles on the unit, shocked back
to pleasantries by the lightning that blew her mind
that morning. Days later, the old rumbling
erupts. She holes up in the ladies' bathroom,
jams the door from inside with a broken mop handle
until her husband leaves the floor.

When a thunderstorm clears the air,
birds shelter among leaves to wait it out.
When volcanoes shake the trees by the roots,
the birds fly up, take shelter in air,
in openness. St. Francis left his house,
throwing his clothes in the street,
stepping through the shelter of his father's shouts.
Three weeks later, Sandy gets a legal separation,
taking to the air, escaping suffocation and lightning.
Last we hear, she's gone back to school.

Lightning can only strike the surface.
Lightning cannot bury a town.
Lightning cannot change the ground.

Constant Watch, Ten-Thirty PM

Darnell Hodges' oxygen tank hums
like a transformer in a lonely alley.
He set his living room on fire
then lay down on the couch to die.
I sit by his door on constant watch,
waiting for shift's end. I breathe in tension
as if it were oxygen, force-fed to me
in clear plastic tubes.

Mr. Heally drags around the corner
of the main hall, his gait
a shuffle to a blues song
out of his distant youth. His eyes open
on a vista of grief, a knowledge that burns
like acid through my routine
fatigue before he disappears
into the lunging shadows of the lounge.

In his room, Hodges heaves labored
breaths, alone with his burned lungs.
It only takes a moment to die,
or see into the heart of things.

Death for Breakfast

I'm feeding Stash in his wheelchair.
Fish-like, he opens his mouth
around the spoon, flecks of corn flakes
spackling his chin: *Cardiac arrest,*
eight east. His hands strain against
the wristlets belted to the steel arms
of the chair. The head nurse runs.
An orderly shoves furniture into the hallway.

Stethoscope swinging like the tail
of a lizard, a doctor enters
from the stairwell door. *Bang-bang,*
the double wheels of the crash cart
lurch off the elevator. The cart speeds by us
with a cadre of nurses, the *swish, swish*
of nyloned thighs down the hall. *Who?*
Stash asks. *822?* The pool players in the lounge
lower their cue sticks like rifles at ease.

Patients, nurses, aides, the janitor
unclogging a toilet— we all watch
the glowing light of the doorway.
Out the window the sun bleeds pale
light like a round wound in clouds,
the white stigmata above the city.

Head down, the doctor emerges,
his stethoscope slung lifeless
over the back of his neck.
The crash cart's wires dangle
like useless hands as a nurse switches off
the heart monitor. Its screen goes gray,
a blank round eye. Stash gazes
down into his soggy cereal.
For a moment, none of us is crazy.

Parables of Perfect Joy

I. *St. Francis' Story*

All the masters of theology in Paris, all the prelates beyond the mountains,
  archbishops, the Kings of France and England have joined the Order.
My friars have gone to the unbelievers and converted them all to the faith.
I heal the sick and perform many miracles.
I tell you perfect joy is not in these things.

I'm returning from Perugia at night in winter.
It's wet, muddy and so cold that icicles form on the hems of my habit and
  keep striking my legs and blood flows from the wounds.
I come to the gate and I knock for a long time.
A friar comes and says, *Go away, Francis. You uneducated fellow.*
I ask again to be let in.
Don't stay with us any more, you crazy man. We don't need you.
Still I stay. *For the love of God won't you let me in?*
I won't, he says. *Go to the Crosiers Place or sleep here in the mud.*
I tell you if I keep patience and don't get angry, that is perfect joy.

II. *One Night On Eight East*

Dr. L's prediction that all psychiatry will be drug-related in twenty years,
  and that medications will cure every patient, comes true now.
All the patients given shock treatments by Dr. R., nicknamed "Redi-kilowatt"
  by the hospital staff, witness forever the light of their own inner being.
Dr. T's belief that methadone for heroin users is just changing staterooms
  on the Titanic is false and all the drug addicts are cured.
The pharmaceutical companies decide not to market their drugs directly to
  patients.
Every patient I meet on the unit is cured simply by talking to me.
Perfect joy is not in these dreams.

It's five to eleven, almost bar-time for me. Arturo Menghini stands in the
hallway in his pajamas.
Please don't do this to me, he says. *I've been good to you guys. Help me
find my room.*
I take him to bed and he says, *Stay with me. Please hold my hand.*
The night nurse tells me to go home.
I ask to stay past my shift. *No* she says. *It's against the rules.*
I ask again, *Let me stay till he falls asleep.*
He has an inoperable brain tumor. There's nothing we can do for him.
Still I say, *Let me stay fifteen minutes.*
If you don't leave, I'll write you up for insubordination.
She hustles away with her angry chart. I stay anyway.
I sit in the darkness, his hand to mine, mine to his.
Late that night it comes to me, through a haze of weariness like an
old memory, a patience that could be exhaustion, but isn't:
unexpected, mysterious. Joy.

The Divine Salt

St. Francis was still dressed as a layman, and for a long time he had been going around Assisi looking contemptible and so mortified that many people thought he was simple-minded, and he was laughed at as a lunatic and driven away with many insults and stones and mud by his relatives and by strangers. Yet being nourished by the divine salt, he bore all the insults and scorn with great patience.

The people saw St. Francis lie on his back
in the dirt of the village street.
He ordered Brother Bernard
to put one foot on his mouth
and one on his neck
and walk over him three times saying,
Lie there you country lout,
you worthless creature.

A great throng of sparrows, doves
and blackbirds gathered in the trees
as St. Francis left the town.
The people saw Francis go to them
and say, *My little bird sisters,*
be careful not to be ungrateful
but strive always to praise God.
And after finishing his sermon
he made the sign of the cross
and gave the birds permission to leave.

Brother Rufino entered Assisi naked.
The people stuck their heads out windows
craning to see. He entered the church,
knelt to pray, then ascended
the pulpit to preach. Soon St. Francis
walked down the street naked,
and the people followed him.

The children and men laughed,
Look, they are doing so much penance,
they have gone crazy.

That night on Mount Alverna,
a flaming Seraph came to St. Francis
in the likeness of a crucified man
to promise him bleeding palms and feet,
a wound in his side streaming
an endless river of suffering. The light
on the mountain shone so bright
into the windows of the village below
that muleteers who were going to Romagna
got up and loaded their mules
thinking the sun had risen.

Driving Home

One morning, I leave the wing, frazzled
from an all-night death watch. Gertie clung
to her frail flame and smoldering,
82-year-old dementia in room 802,
narrow and bare as a monastic cell.
She died at five a.m. of heart failure
after a record stay on the unit.

I pick up a high school senior, hitching,
late for home room, wild-haired,
smart-ass. We compare notes on "house rules,"
patients versus students, locked stairwells
and hall passes, seclusion rooms
and in-school detention. He says, *I'll bet
you don't learn anything there either.*

I want to be equal to his offhand
admiration for what he thinks I do.
At his school, we share a sixties handshake,
grasping wrists, interlocking thumbs.
His hand is warm as igniting kindling.
How to tell him anything without preaching?
So I say, *You learn that you get one life,
and a thousand ways to screw it up.*

■

Family

Lying sick at San Damiano, a fever
weakening his body, already bleeding
from the stigmata's five wounds,
Francis sings a canticle
praising the Father for all creatures.
Brother Sun, you give the light of day.
He speaks in turn to his Brothers Wind and Fire,
his Sisters Moon, Water, and Earth.

A new friar is said to have whispered,
Has Brother Francis lost his mind?

With a stanza for each, Francis
thanks his brothers and sisters,
the elements, who teach us to forgive.
He saves the canticle's end, the final stanza,
for the last Sister, Bodily Death,
the equal of all the others,
as if in forgiveness our bodies learn
to die a little, so we can grow in spirit,

as if poverty is an infinite treasure,
and Death is as beautiful as Mother
Earth with her fruits and flowers,
radiant as Sunlight, chaste as Water,
merry and strong as Fire.